Weird, wild, and wonderful Mammals

By Rosa Inserra

Gareth Stevens
Publishing

Please visit our Web site **www.garethstevens.com**. For a free color catalog of all our high-quality books, call toll free 1-800-542-2595 or fax 1-877-542-2596.

Library of Congress Cataloging-in-Publication Data

Inserra, Rose, 1958-
 Mammals / Rose Inserra.
     p. cm. — (Weird, wild, and wonderful)
 Includes index.
 ISBN 978-1-4339-3573-2 (library binding)
 1. Mammals—Juvenile literature. I. Title.
 QL706.2.I57 2010
 599—dc22

                              2009043972

Published in 2010 by
Gareth Stevens Publishing
111 East 14th Street, Suite 349
New York, NY 10003

© 2010 Blake Publishing

For Gareth Stevens Publishing:
Art Direction: Haley Harasymiw
Editorial Direction: Kerri O'Donnell

Designed in Australia by www.design-ed.com.au

Photography by Kathie Atkinson

Printed in the United States of America

CPSIA compliance information: Batch #CW10GS: For further information contact Gareth Stevens, New York, New York, at 1-800-542-2595.

Contents

What Are Mammals?...................... 4

Spiky Echidnas 6

The Weirdest Mammal.................... 8

Hopping Kangaroos.......................10

Earth Diggers.................................12

Sleepy Koalas 14

Desert Dwellers 16

Night Flyers 18

Elephant Seals 20

Fact File: Types of Mammals........ 22

Glossary 23

For Further Information 24

Index..24

What Are Mammals?

Mammals are found all over the world. Some mammals are truly weird, wild, and wonderful.

Mammals are animals with a backbone. They are warm-blooded animals and have hair, fur, whiskers, or **bristles**. All mammals suckle their young. This means they feed their young on mother's milk.

Fact Bites

Animals with a backbone are called vertebrates.

The blue whale is the world's largest mammal.

Female mammals produce milk to feed their young.

4

There are three groups of mammals.

1. Monotremes

The platypus and echidna are monotremes. These are mammals that lay eggs. They suckle their young from mother's milk.

2. Marsupials

Animals with a pouch are called marsupials. Their young are very tiny when they are born. They live in the pouch until they are more developed. Kangaroos and koalas are marsupials.

3. Placentals

People, bats, cows, mice, and dolphins—as well as lots of other animals—are placental mammals. The baby grows inside the mother's body until it is ready to be born.

A kangaroo with its **joey** in its pouch

A mouse with its newborn babies

5

Spiky Echidnas

The echidna is a monotreme that lays eggs. It lives in Australia, Tasmania, and New Guinea. The long spines protect the echidna from **predators**.

Only its stomach is soft and furry. Between the spines is rough hair. This keeps the echidna warm in winter and cool in summer.

The short-beaked echidna has long, sharp spines that scare off predators.

Echidnas can feel **vibrations** and have wonderful hearing. This makes it easy for them to find bugs and other echidnas.

The echidna has a long **snout** to reach into ant and termite nests. It licks up the bugs with its long, sticky tongue.

When it is time to have babies, the female echidna lays one egg in her pouch. After 10 days, the egg **hatches**.

The echidna licks up insects from termite and ant nests.

When an echidna is scared, it digs into the ground or rolls up into a spiky ball.

A baby echidna is called a puggle.

7

The Weirdest Mammal

What mammal has a duck's bill, a large flat tail, a poisonous spike, and a seal's body? It's a platypus. What a weird mix!

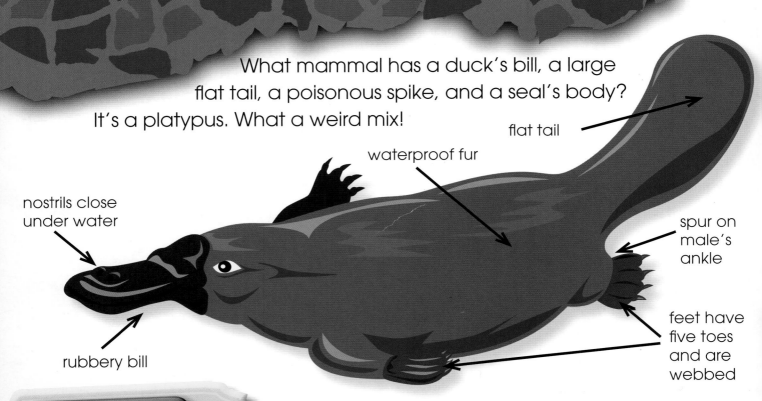

flat tail

waterproof fur

nostrils close under water

rubbery bill

spur on male's ankle

feet have five toes and are webbed

Fact Bite

Baby platypuses drink milk that oozes from a patch on the mother's skin.

Like the echidna, the platypus is a monotreme. It has **webbed** feet and wonderful waterproof fur. Its bill is rubbery and has special senses. It can feel vibrations from its favorite foods— worms, bugs, shrimp, and crayfish.

Platypuses store food in pouches in their cheeks.

The platypus lives in the Australian wild on the banks of creeks, streams, ponds, and rivers. Platypuses spend most of their time swimming. They rest in their **burrows**.

The male has a poisonous spike called a spur on each hind leg. These are used for fighting other males.

9

Hopping Kangaroos

Kangaroos are marsupials that live in Australia and New Guinea. They belong to the macropod family. "Macropod" means "big footed."

The kangaroo hops on its strong hind legs. It can hop very fast. Its wonderful tail is thick and heavy. This helps it balance when hopping. There are many types of kangaroos. Some can grow taller than a person. Some, such as the musky-rat kangaroo, are only as big as a guinea pig.

Western grey kangaroos

Fact Bites

A male kangaroo is called a buck.

A female kangaroo is called a doe.

A baby kangaroo is called a joey.

A kangaroo can hop up to 35 miles (55 km) per hour. That's as fast as a car driving in the street.

Kangaroos live in groups called mobs. Moving around in mobs is safer than being alone. Kangaroos are often hunted by foxes, **feral** dogs, and **dingoes**.

Kangaroos feed at night. They are plant-eaters, or herbivores. They eat grass, leaves, and tree shoots.

During the day, kangaroos rest in the shade. They pant and lick their arms to keep cool.

This wallaby joey is growing quite big. Its mother's pouch stretches to fit the joey as it grows.

Wombats are Australian marsupials. They live in bushy areas and also in dry, hot places. Wombats are **nocturnal**. They feed at night for 3 to 8 hours. During the day, wombats stay in underground burrows. Wombats eat **native** grasses, roots, and bushes.

Their strong claws make them wonderful diggers. They dig long burrows that have lots of smaller tunnels. This makes it easy for wombats to move around underground.

The wombat is the largest marsupial that digs burrows.

Fact Bite

Wombats can survive fires aboveground if they stay in their burrows.

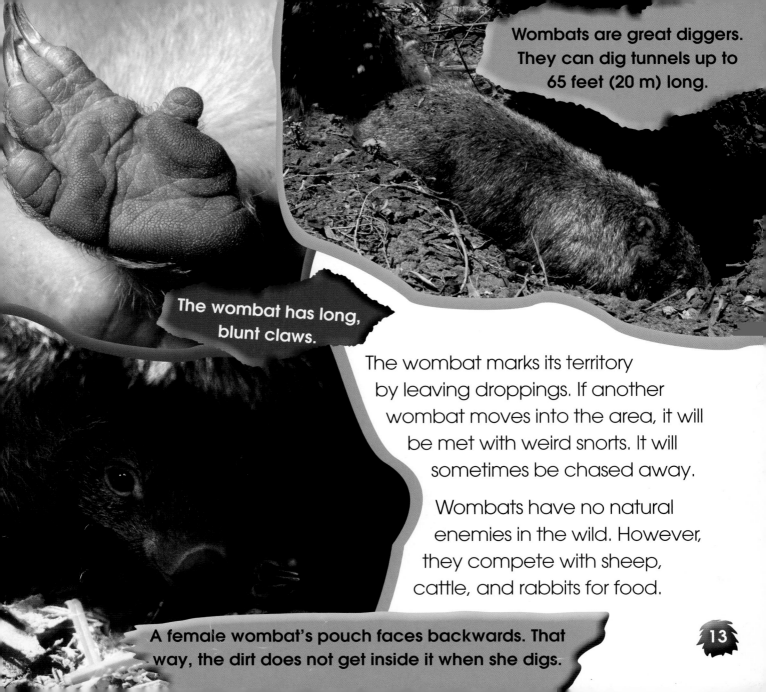

Wombats are great diggers. They can dig tunnels up to 65 feet (20 m) long.

The wombat has long, blunt claws.

The wombat marks its territory by leaving droppings. If another wombat moves into the area, it will be met with weird snorts. It will sometimes be chased away.

Wombats have no natural enemies in the wild. However, they compete with sheep, cattle, and rabbits for food.

A female wombat's pouch faces backwards. That way, the dirt does not get inside it when she digs.

Sleepy Koalas

Koalas are Australian marsupials. They are not bears! They are found in many areas, such as forests, near the coast, and in Australian wilderness called bushland. Koalas are wonderful climbers and live in trees. They also love to sleep.

Koalas sleep and rest for about 20 hours a day!

A baby koala is called a joey.

Koalas only eat leaves from special eucalyptus trees. An adult koala can eat over 2 pounds (1 kg) of leaves each day. It doesn't need to drink. A koala gets water from the leaves.

The koala's leaf diet does not give it much energy. That's why koalas are only active for about 4 hours a day. Koalas are active at night and in the early morning.

Koalas only come down to the ground to change trees.

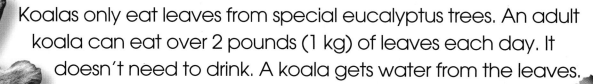

Koalas use their strong claws to climb high in eucalyptus trees.

Fact Bites

Koalas make wild squeals and grunts to talk to each other.

The fur on the koala's bottom is extra thick. It acts like a cushion. It makes it more comfortable for koalas to sit on hard branches.

A koala eating eucalyptus leaves

15

Desert Dwellers

In the desert, foxes hunt marsupials for food.

The desert is a very dry place. There is little water and not much food for mammals. Those that live there act in special ways that suit this **habitat**.

In summer, the Australian desert is very hot during the day. Desert mammals have to find shelter from the sun. They dig burrows under the sand. There they can rest and stay cool.

Bilbies are marsupials that live in the desert. They have sharp claws to help them dig.

Fact Bites

Foxes were brought to Australia by settlers from Europe.

There are only a small number of bilbies left in the wild.

Desert marsupials are nocturnal. They come out at night to eat and hunt. It's much cooler then. They like to feed on bugs, fungi, wild fruits, spiders, seeds, and grasses. Desert marsupials get all the water they need from their food. They don't have to drink water.

The spinifex hopping-mouse gets the water it needs from its food.

The fat-tailed marsupial mouse stores fat in its tail. This helps it survive when there is no food around.

Foxes and feral cats live in the desert, too. At night, they hunt desert marsupials for food. The marsupial mouse and the bilby use their burrows to get away from these hunters.

17

Night Flyers

The flying fox wraps itself up to go to sleep.

Flying foxes are not foxes at all. These weird-looking mammals are large fruit bats. They hang upside down in trees. The grey-headed flying fox is the largest fruit bat. It can weigh more than 2 pounds (1 kg).

Flying foxes are nocturnal mammals. They search for food at night. They have large eyes that can see during the day and at night. This makes it easier to find their favorite foods. They like to eat gum blossoms, fruits, **nectar**, and **pollen** from native trees.

Flying foxes are found in Asia, Indonesia, Madagascar, and Australia.

The flying fox hangs by long thumbs on its wrists. Its legs are too weak to stand on.

Fact Bites

Bats are the only mammals that can fly.

The flying fox's wings are made up of skin stretched over its arms and fingers.

Flying foxes also use their wonderful sense of smell to find food. They search for food in parks, gardens, backyards, and forests. Flying foxes can travel up to 30 miles (50 k) to find food.

During the day, flying foxes **roost** in trees. A **colony** is made up of many thousands of flying foxes. It's wild and noisy out there!

19

Elephant Seals

Most mammals live on land, but some live in the sea. They are called **marine** mammals. Seals are marine mammals that belong to a group called pinnipeds. This means "fin foot." They spend some time on land and use their fins like feet.

Male elephant seals look a bit like elephants. They're very large and have a short trunk.

This elephant seal is using its "fingernails" to groom itself.

Adult male elephant seals can weigh over 8,000 pounds (3,600 kg). That is the size of a land elephant or a whale.

Elephant seals feed mainly on squid and fish.

A harem is made up of a group of about 50 females with their pups.

Elephant seals are found on land during the breeding season. This is the time when they **mate** and have babies. They also return to land when it is time to shed their fur. The rest of their time is spent in the sea.

Elephant seals have a thick layer of **blubber**. This keeps them warm. They can stay underwater for up to 2 hours and not get cold.

Elephant seals breed in groups called harems. Male elephant seals have wild fights over who controls the harem.

The male's trunk helps to carry the sound of its loud roar.

These young males don't have trunks yet.

Fact File: Types of Mammals

How do you recognize a mammal? Look in the mirror. You are a mammal. All humans are.

You are warm-blooded.

You have hair.

You were fed on milk when you were a baby.

Mammal Groups		
Monotremes (lay eggs)	**Marsupials (have a pouch)**	**Placentals (grow inside the mother)**
platypus	koala	dolphin
echidna	kangaroo	dingo
	possum	flying fox
	tasmanian devil	seal
	wombat	cow
		human
		dog

Glossary

blubber — a kind of fat that keeps seals, walruses, and whales warm

bristles — thick, stiff hairs

burrows — holes underground

colony — a large group of animals that live together

dingoes — wild dogs of Australia

feral — having once lived with people but gone back to the wild

habitat — a place where animals usually live

hatch — to come out of an egg

joey — a baby marsupial

marine — belonging to the ocean

mate — to make babies

native — something that has always belonged to that place

nectar — a sweet liquid from plants

nocturnal — active at night

pollen — very tiny seeds carried by the wind

predators — animals that kill other animals for food

roost — to settle down for rest or sleep

snout — a long nose

vibrations — shaky movements

webbed — having thin skin between toes

For Further Information

Books

Solway, Andrew. *Classifying Mammals.* Chicago: Heinemann-Raintree, 2009.

Taylor, Barbara. *Planet Animal: Mammals.* London: Carlton Books, 2010.

Web Sites

National Geographic: Mammals
http://animals.nationalgeographic.com/animals/mammals.html

Small Mammal Facts: National Zoo
http://nationalzoo.si.edu/Animals/SmallMammals/smfactsheets.cfm

Publisher's note to educators and parents: Our editors have carefully reviewed these Web sites to ensure that they are suitable for students. Many Web sites change frequently, however, and we cannot guarantee that a site's future contents will continue to meet our high standards of quality and educational value. Be advised that students should be closely supervised whenever they access the Internet.

Index

bats 5, 18, 19

bilbies 16, 17

burrows 9, 12, 16, 17

desert 16, 17

echidnas 5, 6, 7, 8, 22

eggs 5, 6, 7, 22

elephant seals 20, 21

flying foxes 18, 19, 22

foxes 11, 16, 17, 18

herbivores 11

joey 5, 10, 11, 14

kangaroos 5, 10, 11, 22

koalas 5, 14, 15, 22

macropod 10

marine mammals 20

marsupial mouse 17

marsupials 5, 10, 12, 14, 16, 17, 22

milk 4, 5, 8, 22

monotremes 5, 6, 8, 22

nectar 18

nocturnal 12, 17, 18

placentals 5, 22

platypuses 5, 8, 9, 22

pollen 18

pouches 5, 7, 9, 11, 13, 22

puggle 7

spinifex hopping-mouse 17

suckle 4, 5

wallaby 11

whale 4, 21

wombats 12, 13, 22